Mummies

The Valley of the Kings:

Egypt's Greatest Mummies

by Michael Burgan

Consultant:

Dr. Salima Ikram

Department of Egyptology

American University in Cairo

Cairo, Egypt

Capstone
press

Mankato, Minnesota

Edge Books are published by Capstone Press,
151 Good Counsel Drive, P.O. Box 669, Mankato, Minnesota 56002.
www.capstonepress.com

Library of Congress Cataloging-in-Publication Data
Burgan, Michael.
    The valley of the Kings: Egypt's greatest mummies / by Michael Burgan.
        p. cm.—(Edge Books: Mummies.)
    Includes bibliographical references and index.
    ISBN 0-7368-3772-8 (hardcover)
    1. Valley of the Kings (Egypt)—Juvenile literature. 2. Tombs—Egypt—Valley of
the Kings—Juvenile literature. 3. Mummies—Egypt—Valley of the Kings—Juvenile
literature. I. Title. II. Series.
DT73.B44B87 2005
932—dc22   2004010552

Summary: Describes the Valley of the Kings, the tombs and mummies found there,
and what scientists have learned from the valley's discoveries.

Editorial Credits
Carrie A. Braulick, editor; Kia Adams, set designer; Jennifer Bergstrom, book designer;
    Kelly Garvin, photo researcher; Scott Thoms, photo editor

Photo Credits
Art Resource, NY/Erich Lessing, 12; Scala, cover
Corbis/Bettmann, 17; Gianni Dagli Orti, 23; Nathan Benn, 15; Reuters/Aladin Abdel
    Naby, 10; Robert Holmes, 28; Roger Wood, 11, 20; Sandro Vannini, 24
Getty Images/Discovery Channel, 26; Hulton Archive, 18
Mary Evans Picture Library/Douglas Dickins, 19
Woodfin Camp & Associates Inc./Barry Iverson, 4, 7

**Capstone Press thanks Carolyn Graves-Brown, Egypt Centre, University of Wales
Swansea, for her assistance in preparing this book.**

1 2 3 4 5 6 10 09 08 07 06 05

Table of Contents

Learn About:

- Kent Weeks
- KV 5 discoveries
- Pyramids of Egypt

Rubble filled KV 5, but Kent Weeks still made important discoveries there.

Chapter One

Discovery of a Tomb

In 1995, Kent Weeks dug through rubble that blocked a tomb's doorway. Weeks and other archaeologists were exploring Egypt's Valley of the Kings. Weeks expected to find a small room on the other side of the doorway. Instead, he found a long hallway lined with doorways. The doorways led to more halls and rooms.

The scientists found more than 130 rooms in the tomb. Ancient Egyptian pottery, statues, and thousands of other objects filled the rooms. The scientists even found human skulls.

The tomb Weeks explored is called KV 5. It is the largest tomb ever discovered in the Valley of the Kings. Scientists believe KV 5 was built for the sons of Ramses II. Ramses II was an ancient Egyptian king, or pharaoh. Ramses II had at least 50 sons. Some scientists think he may have had more than 100 sons.

Ancient Egyptian Beliefs

The ancient Egyptians made millions of dead bodies into mummies. They believed spirits inside their bodies could live in an afterworld only if their bodies were preserved. Ancient Egyptians put the mummies in tombs.

Ancient Egyptians also thought spirits needed supplies for the afterworld. They stored food, clothes, furniture, and other objects in tombs. Tombs of the pharaohs held the most valuable objects. These tombs held jewelry, gold statues, and other treasures.

EDGE FACT

In the early 1800s, people destroyed thousands of ancient Egyptian mummies. They ground up the mummies into powder. Europeans used the powder as medicine.

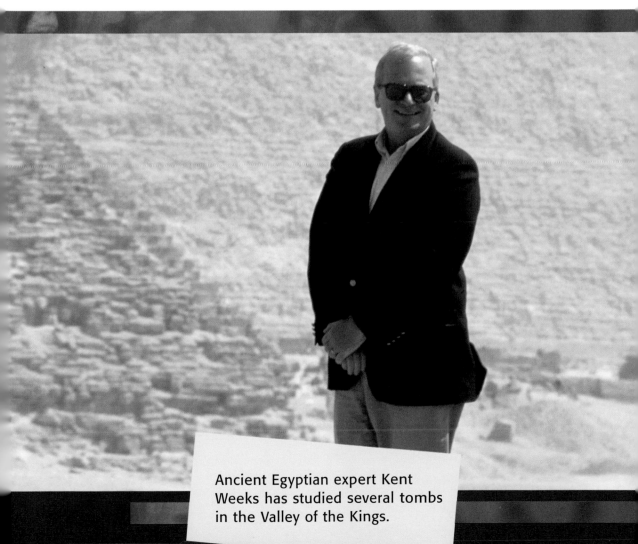

Ancient Egyptian expert Kent Weeks has studied several tombs in the Valley of the Kings.

Some Tombs in the Valley of the Kings

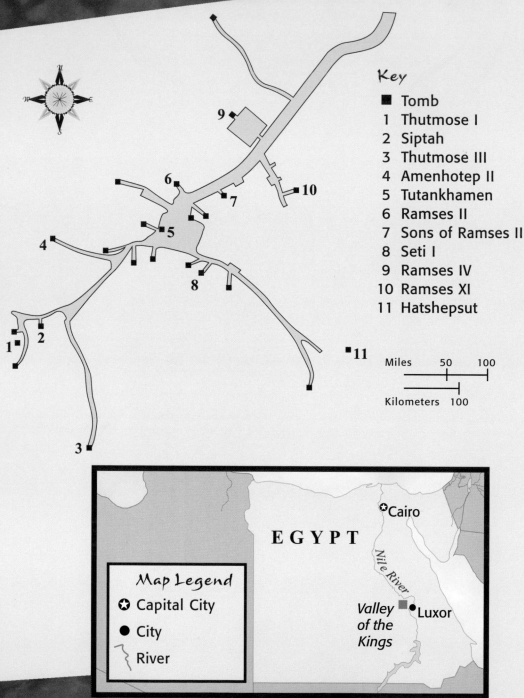

Key

■ Tomb
1 Thutmose I
2 Siptah
3 Thutmose III
4 Amenhotep II
5 Tutankhamen
6 Ramses II
7 Sons of Ramses II
8 Seti I
9 Ramses IV
10 Ramses XI
11 Hatshepsut

Miles   50   100

Kilometers   100

Cairo

EGYPT

Nile River

Valley of the Kings   Luxor

Map Legend

✪ Capital City

● City

River

A New Place for Tombs

Early pharaohs were buried in large stone pyramids. Many of the large pyramids were built during a time period of ancient Egypt called the Old Kingdom. This period took place about 3,700 to 4,700 years ago.

About 3,000 to 3,500 years ago, a period called the New Kingdom began. The New Kingdom pharaohs wanted different tombs. The large pyramids were hard to guard. Robbers often stole valuable objects from them.

The New Kingdom pharaohs chose to be buried in tombs cut into the sides of hills. The pharaohs chose a valley near the city of Thebes for the tombs' location. Thebes was an important religious center in southern Egypt. Today, the ruins of this ancient city are near Luxor. The valley the pharaohs chose had only one entrance. This feature made it easier for the ancient Egyptians to guard.

The ancient Egyptians sometimes called the valley "The Great Place." Today, it is called the Valley of the Kings.

Many tombs in the Valley of the Kings held mummies. Scientists believe this mummy is pharaoh Ramses I.

About the Valley

Sixty-two tombs have been found in the Valley of the Kings. Most of these tombs were built for pharaohs. Others were for important government officials.

Scientists have found mummies in at least 20 of the tombs. Many mummies found in and near the valley were pharaohs. These royal mummies were usually the most important discoveries.

The Valley of the Queens

Pharaohs often had many wives. A few ancient Egyptian queens were buried with their husbands in the Valley of the Kings. Many more were buried in a nearby area known as the Valley of the Queens. Many of the pharaohs' children also were buried there. The ancient Egyptians called this valley "The Place of Beauty." Scientists have found at least 90 tombs in the Valley of the Queens. One of the largest tombs belonged to Nefertari. She was a wife of Ramses II.

Nefertari's tomb

Many small paths wind through the Valley of the Kings.

Chapter Two

Inside the Valley

The Valley of the Kings has one main road. It enters the valley at the northern end. Smaller paths branch off this road. Most pharaohs' tombs were built near the smaller paths.

Scientists labeled each tomb in the valley. Tombs found in the eastern part begin with the letters "KV." Tombs in the western part begin with the letters "WV." Most numbers after the letters show the order in which the tombs were found.

Finding the Tombs

People have explored the Valley of the Kings for hundreds of years. In 1739, Englishman Richard Pococke made the first map of the valley. It included 18 tombs.

In the 1800s, archaeologists found more tombs. Italian Giovanni Belzoni made the first major discovery in 1817. He found pharaoh Seti I's tomb, KV 17. This pharaoh is also known as Sethos I.

In 1881, Egyptians discovered a tomb near the valley in an area known as Deir el-Bahri. The tomb held about 40 royal mummies. One of the mummies was Ramses II. Ramses II built more statues and temples than any other pharaoh. The tomb's discovery attracted more explorers to the valley.

In 1899, French archaeologist Victor Loret found KV 38. Scientists believe Thutmose III built this tomb for his grandfather, Thutmose I.

Howard Carter uncovered KV 62 in 1922. It belonged to King Tutankhamen. Today, this pharaoh is sometimes called King Tut. No tomb has been discovered since King Tut's tomb.

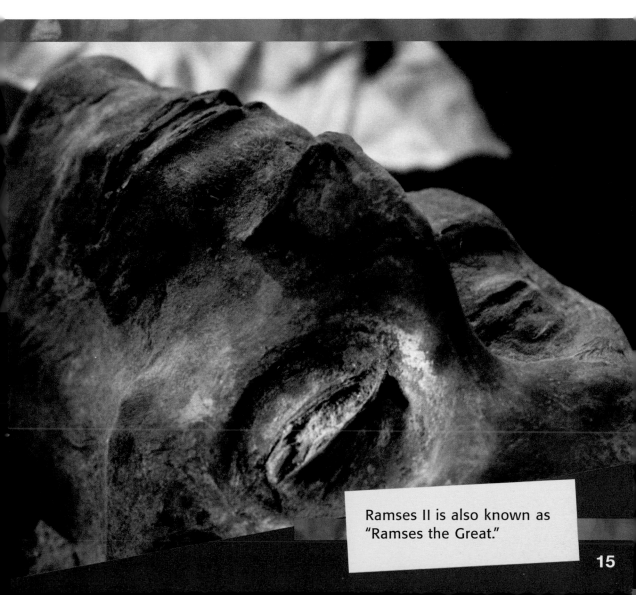

Ramses II is also known as "Ramses the Great."

Dynasties

The pharaohs belonged to dynasties. A group of pharaohs who were related made up a dynasty. A king's son or another relative usually became pharaoh when a king died. Scientists believe ancient Egypt had about 30 dynasties.

Pharaohs from three dynasties are buried in the Valley of the Kings. The pharaohs of the 18th dynasty are farthest south. Tombs of the 19th dynasty kings are mainly in the middle section. Most members of the 20th dynasty are buried at the northern end of the valley.

King Seti I ruled during the 19th dynasty.
His mummy was discovered in Deir el-Bahri
in 1881.

Pharaohs' Tombs

Each tomb has features that make it valuable to scientists. King Tut's tomb was one of the most important tombs ever found. Scientists found more treasures there than in any other tomb in the valley.

Animal Mummies

The ancient Egyptians mummified millions of animals. Some animal mummies were pets. Others were sacrifices to the gods or sacred animals. Scientists have found mummies of monkeys, crocodiles, cats, hawks, and other animals. Most of these mummies were buried in tombs in animal cemeteries. In the Valley of the Kings, tombs KV 50 and KV 51 held animal mummies.

In 2001, the remains of a lion were found near a tomb scientists believe was for King Tut's nurse. Some scientists believe the discovery shows that lions were sacred animals in ancient Egypt.

Cat mummies

The oldest tomb in the Valley of the Kings is probably KV 20. It is far east of the valley's main road. Pharaoh Thutmose I built this tomb. His daughter Hatshepsut was buried there.

The last tomb cut in the valley was KV 4. It belonged to Ramses XI. But the pharaoh was never buried there. His mummy has not been found.

Seti I's tomb is the valley's longest. The 450-foot (137-meter) tomb is covered with colorful paintings. It was the first tomb discovered with paintings in every room.

The walls of Seti I's tomb are covered in detailed paintings.

Learn About:

- Tomb builders
- Dangers of tomb building
- Tomb artwork

The tomb builders lived just outside the valley in Deir el-Medina.

Chapter Three
Building the Valley of the Kings

Building a tomb in the Valley of the Kings was a large, difficult project. After a location was chosen for a pharaoh's tomb, designers planned the location of the tomb's rooms. Between 30 and 120 workers built a tomb.

The workers who built the tombs during the 18th dynasty were called "Servants in the Great Place." Later, workers were called "Servants in the Place of Truth."

The Tomb Builders

The tomb builders lived in a small village outside the Valley of the Kings called Deir el-Medina. The workers lived with their families. The village had about 70 homes and several workshops. Workers walked from the village to the valley on a mountain path.

Tomb builders divided up the work. Two teams usually worked on each tomb. A small group of leaders was in charge of each team. Some workers cut and dug the tombs with hard stone tools. Others carried away the rubble left behind. The work usually took several years.

The workers built tombs mainly for pharaohs and the pharaohs' relatives. In their spare time, they could build their own tombs.

The builders faced hard, dangerous conditions inside the tombs. The tombs were hot. Cutting the tombs filled the air with dust. Rock ceilings could fall and kill everyone underneath.

The ancient Egyptians made metal and stone tools for digging into the valley's rocks.

Tomb workers left behind records of their lives. Scientists have found letters and poetry written by the workers. Some discoveries list names of the workers and their family members.

Parts of the Book of the Dead
were sometimes painted on
tomb walls.

Decorating the Tombs

After a tomb was cut, workers often covered the walls with plaster. This material made the walls smooth. The tomb builders or skilled artists then decorated the walls with paintings or carvings.

Religious scenes or chapters from books were common in tomb artwork. The scenes often included gods and the tomb's owner. Scenes from the Book of the Dead were sometimes shown. The Book of the Dead was filled with magical spells. The spells were meant to help spirits safely reach the afterworld.

Scientists carefully study the mummies of the Valley of the Kings.

Chapter Four

Mysteries Solved

Each discovery from the Valley of the Kings is important to scientists. Scientists send most objects to museums to keep them safe.

Some objects teach scientists how the ancient Egyptians lived. Musical instruments and games show some of their activities. Chariot parts show how they traveled.

Inside the Mummies

X-rays and CT scans show scientists the insides of mummies. In 1968, scientists took an x-ray of King Tut's skull. The picture showed that the bone behind King Tut's left ear was thinner than other parts of his skull. Scientists believe a blow to this spot might have caused his death.

Each year, thousands of tourists come to the Valley of the Kings.

Some mummies show signs of bad health or disease. Scientists believe Amenhotep III was overweight. Many pharaohs seemed to have a disease called arthritis. This painful disease affects the joints where bones meet. The pharaoh Siptah's right leg was shorter than his left leg. Scientists believe a disease called polio might have caused this condition.

The Valley Today

Archaeologists continue to study the tombs in the Valley of the Kings. They are still exploring KV 5. They expect to find many more rooms in this huge tomb.

Scientists want to make sure the tombs stay in good condition. Thousands of people visit the Valley of the Kings each year. Scientists plan programs to clean up trash left by the tourists. Some scientists preserve tomb paintings. These efforts will help keep the tombs open for future visitors of the valley.

Glossary

archaeologist (ar-kee-OL-uh-jist)—a scientist who searches for and studies the items left behind by ancient people to learn about the past

chariot (CHAIR-ee-uht)—a small vehicle pulled by a horse

dynasty (DYE-nuh-stee)—a group of rulers from the same family or with another connection to each other

pharaoh (FAIR-oh)—a king of ancient Egypt

plaster (PLASS-tur)—a substance made of lime, sand, and water

polio (POH-lee-oh)—a disease that attacks the brain and spinal chord

pyramid (PIHR-uh-mid)—a large triangle-shaped ancient Egyptian tomb with four sides

spirit (SPIHR-it)—the invisible part of a person that many people believe contains thoughts and feelings; ancient Egyptians believed the spirit left the body after death and traveled to another world.

tomb (TOOM)—a grave, room, or building that holds a dead body

x-ray (EKS-ray)—a picture of the inside of a body

Read More

Berger, Melvin, and Gilda Berger. *Mummies of the Pharaohs: Exploring the Valley of the Kings.* Washington, D.C.: National Geographic Society, 2001.

Malam, John. *Mummies and the Secrets of Ancient Egypt.* Secret Worlds. New York: DK Publishing, 2001.

Smith, Stuart Tyson, and Nancy Stone Bernard. *Valley of the Kings.* Digging for the Past. New York: Oxford University Press, 2002.

Internet Sites

FactHound offers a safe, fun way to find Internet sites related to this book. All of the sites on FactHound have been researched by our staff.

Here's how:

1. Visit *www.facthound.com*
2. Type in this special code **0736837728** for age-appropriate sites. Or enter a search word related to this book for a more general search.
3. Click on the **Fetch It** button.

FactHound will fetch the best sites for you!

Index